St Cuthbert's Way

from Melrose to Lindisfarne
with high-level option over the Cheviot

Ronald Turnbull

Rucksack Readers

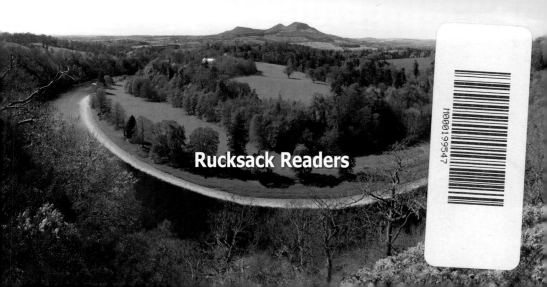

St Cuthbert's Way from Melrose to Lindisfarne

First published 2010, reprinted with revisions 2016

Rucksack Readers, 6 Old Church Lane, Edinburgh, EH15 3PX

Telephone   +44/0 131 661 0262
Email   info@rucsacs.com
Website   **www.rucsacs.com**

Designed in Scotland by Ian Clydesdale (*www.workhorse.co.uk*)
Printed in the UK by Ashford Colour Press on rainproof, biodegradable paper

Maps © Stirling Surveys 2010 based on pre-1958 Ordnance Survey material, updated from original field surveys made by the author in 2009 and the publisher in 2016, and from aerial photographs by kind permission of RCAHMS.

Publisher's note

All information was checked prior to publication. However, changes are inevitable: take local advice and look out for waymarkers and other signage e.g. for diversions. Walkers are advised to check two websites for updates before setting out: **www.stcuthbertsway.info** and **www.rucsacs.com/books/scw/**.

A few parts of the Way are fairly remote, and the weather is unpredictable year-round. In mist or low cloud, competence with map and compass will be useful. The high-level Cheviot option is very remote and exposed, and needs competent navigation in any conditions. You are responsible for your own safety and for ensuring that your clothing, food and equipment are suited to your needs. The publisher accepts no liability for any ill-health, accident or loss arising directly or indirectly from reading this book.

Feedback is welcome and will be rewarded.

We are grateful to readers for their comments and suggestions. All feedback will be followed up, and readers whose comments lead to changes will be entitled to claim a free copy of our next edition upon publication. Please send emails to **info@rucsacs.com**.

St Cuthbert's Way: contents

Introduction

Study St Cuthbert's Way on the map, and you may expect a slightly tame walk with a tendency to stay at or below the 300m contour, a selection of Borders abbeys, a stretch of the Tweed and a final section apparently underwater.

What the map doesn't prepare you for is the sheer charm of this comparatively short path. Its hills may be small, but they are certainly hilly: from the volcanic knobs of the Eildons clothed in lurid gorse and inhabited by the Queen of Elfland herself to the shapely foothills of the Cheviots, each one cloaked with steep grass and crowned with a hill fort.

Then there are the small woods, some of open pine, some scrubby, some verging on jungle. There are the countless streams, where wild garlic shines among the brown gloom. Even the short road section surprised me: north-east of Wooler a dead rabbit slid along the tarmac, apparently self-propelled – actually pulled by a stoat considerably smaller than itself.

There's much to enjoy along the Way, but even so, you'll be glad when it's over – glad because you've arrived at Lindisfarne. The 'underwater' section across the mudflats of the Pilgrims' Path is unique in British long-distance walking. And the Holy Island of Lindisfarne is one of the country's most magical places.

Many come to St Cuthbert's Way because it is quite short. Many will finish this charming path wishing it were a whole lot longer.

Above Melrose, path onto the Eildons

Planning and preparation

From the red stone village of Melrose, the Way heads straight up to the 300m contour on the volcanic Eildons. After a half-day along the great River Tweed, it strikes south-east across pastureland and through small woods; first along the line of Roman Dere Street, then climbing gradually through more hilly grassland.

After Morebattle the going gets steeper. You'll climb to well above 300m (1000ft) on Wideopen Hill, and (having now entered England) return to this height across the shapely foothills and heather moors of the Cheviots. From Wooler, lower moorland mixed with arable fields and forestry plantation leads you out to the sea. The final crossing to Lindisfarne is made by road causeway or, more adventurously, on the ancient Pilgrims' Path across 2½ miles (4km) of tidal mud.

Through all this variety, the going underfoot is, on the whole, gentle. Here are no bogs, heather-bashing or harsh, stony paths. After the first climb from Melrose, the slopes are neither steep nor unduly long and the Way never ventures above 370m (1210ft). Over the 62 miles (100km), your total ascent is a modest 2250m (7400ft) – increasing to 2750m (9000ft) if you take the ambitious Cheviot option. But because so many paths are grassy, the route does require some care in navigation compared with more frequented, well-worn footpaths.

The Way is normally walked eastwards, from Melrose to Lindisfarne, echoing the progression of St Cuthbert's life: see page 17. On a practical note, wet weather usually arrives from the south-west, so it's more likely to be at your back. More important, this direction makes Lindisfarne the culmination of your walk.

Best time of year and weather

The Way can be walked enjoyably at any time between March and October. The wildflowers are at their best in May and June, and the weather tends to be kind. May to July is the nesting season for sea-birds of Lindisfarne and the Farne Islands. July and August are holiday months, with Scottish schools breaking for the summer at the start of July. The Way, though never crowded, will be at its busiest in those two months. They also have hazy summer light and some inconvenience from biting insects, so are not ideal. Autumn colours are at their finest in late October, and autumn brings thousands of wading birds to Lindisfarne.

If you are an experienced walker and don't mind a bit of cold and wet, you could walk the Way in mid-winter. Expect eight hours of daylight (or even less), some very muddy paths and a shortage of accommodation. When the sun does come out, winter light over the hills and sea can be magical.

On average, the eastern side of the UK is drier and sunnier than the west. But British weather is seldom average. Expect at least some sunshine, and also some rain, on your walk. Continuous heavy rain all day long is rare, but not unknown.

Previous experience

If you've never tackled a long-distance walk before, don't worry: St Cuthbert's Way is an ideal choice. The distances between accommodation points are modest; the terrain mostly has sound surfaces; the gradients are steady with only the odd rough, boggy or steep section; and the waymarking is mostly good, although there are places where you need to be alert.

Sound preparation and planning will help you to enjoy the experience to the full. Inexperienced walkers may find it more enjoyable, as well as safer, to have company. Ideally go with somebody who can use a map and compass, or even attach yourself to an organised group. Note that the Cheviot option is considerably more demanding, both physically and in terms of navigation, than the main Way. It uses unmarked paths over high hills which are exposed to bad weather and hill fog: see pages 48-51.

Book your accommodation well in advance and be realistic in committing yourself to daily distances. In the weeks before, do several all-day walks, if possible on consecutive days, to test your footwear, waterproofs and fitness. Obtain our *Notes for novices* which cover choosing and buying gear: see page 62

Altitude profile of the Way, and the Cheviot option (shown in red)

Throughout this book, altitude profiles are shown with bands of colour, each band representing 50 metres (164 ft).

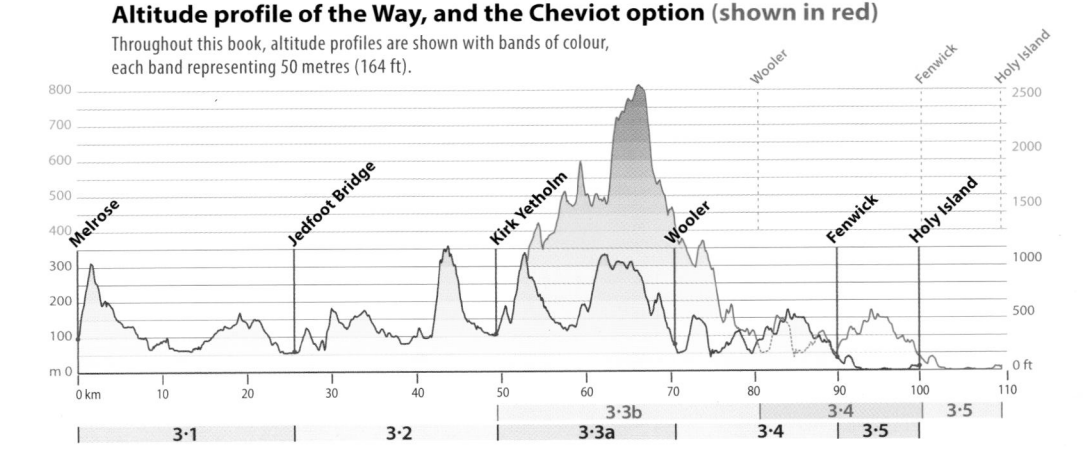

How long will it take?

A strong, fit walker in a hurry could snatch the route in a 3-day long weekend – though getting home from Lindisfarne may add to that. But making a proper holiday of it over five or six days allows time to visit at least one of the ruined abbeys, to explore Melrose and Wooler, and especially to linger on Lindisfarne.

The table presents the distances for a five-day walk. You can add rest days and split the longer days further: see the facilities table. But if you want to extend the actual walking over more than six days, then you'll be dependent on places with a single B&B, which may be full – notably Hethpool, where Hethpool House is the only accommodation between Kirk Yetholm and Wooler.

Table 1: Distances and overnight stops (5-day walk)

section	place	miles	km
	Melrose		
3·1		16	26
	Jedfoot Bridge		
3·2		15	24
	Kirk Yetholm		
3·3a*		13	21
	Wooler		
3·3b	*extra via Cheviot option	+5	+8
3·4		12	19½
	Fenwick		
3·5		6	9½
	Holy Island		
	Total	**62** (67)	**100** (108)

To this you must add time for Holy Island itself. Access across the causeway is possible only during two 8-hour periods in any 24 hours, depending on the tides. The Pilgrims' Path is even more limited: see page 11. Rather than hurrying on and off the island on a single tide, it's better to linger overnight. The tourist tide retreats as the sea advances, making Lindisfarne into a proper island. The sea and the seals approach the shoreline, and evening light plays on the castle walls.

However, accommodation on the island is not of the cheapest, and camping is not allowed. So some may prefer to spend a daytime high tide on the island, before an overnight at Beal or Fenwick, convenient for a morning bus.

Table 2: Facilities along the Way

section	place	distance offroute		B&B/ hotel	hostel	camping	shop	pub, café
	Galashiels	4½mi	7km	✔			✔	✔
3·1	Melrose			✔		✔	✔	✔
3·1	Newtown St Boswells			✔			✔	✔
3·1	St Boswells			✔			✔	✔
3·1	Ancrum	½mi	1km	✔			✔	✔
3·1	Harestanes/Monteviot							✔
3·2	Jedfoot Bridge/Mounthooly							✔
3·2	Jedburgh	2½mi	4km	✔		✔	✔	✔
3·2	Morebattle			✔			✔	✔
3·2	Town Yetholm			✔		✔	✔	✔
3·3	Kirk Yetholm			✔	✔			✔
3·3a	Hethpool			✔				
3·4	Wooler			✔	✔	✔	✔	✔
3·4	East Horton			✔				
3·4	Spylaw Farm			✔				
3·5	Fenwick			✔				
3·5	West Kyloe	1mi	1·6km			✔		
3·5	Beal	1½mi	2½km	✔			✔	✔
3·5	Holy Island village			✔			✔	✔

It's also worth spending time in Melrose at the start, to explore its abbey and perhaps also to visit Abbotsford House nearby: see page 29. At St Boswells, note that Dryburgh Abbey is not visible from the Way: the short diversion across the river Tweed takes an extra hour or so to visit it. A half-day could also be spent in Jedburgh with its abbey, castle, and royal house.

Two further extensions could be considered. Before the start of the walk, Galashiels offers more accommodation choices than Melrose, and all Edinburgh trains stop there (four minutes short of Melrose). After staying in Galashiels, you could head south from the station to pick up the Southern Upland Way on Elm Row, and follow waymarkers for about 8km (5 miles) to reach Melrose. And 26km into the walk, many will prefer to hike the 4km to Jedburgh's shops, pubs and abbey, rather than arrange a taxi from Harestanes Visitor Centre or take a bus from Ancrum: see page 36.

The final option, for the adventurous, is the mountain route over the Cheviot. At 815m (2674ft) this is the summit of the Cheviot range, and of Eastern England. The ascent from Yetholm, waymarked as part of the Pennine Way, is on a grassy path. The descent is on peaty heather paths and 4x4 tracks. If overnighting at Yetholm, you can postpone your final decision about this option until the morning's weather forecast. The hilltop route is slightly longer, and much more strenuous (450m more ascent) than the Way itself, and it takes about 3 hours longer.

Accommodation and supplies

Accommodation along the way is adequate, but not abundant. You are strongly advised to book in advance, even in the off season. A fishing party or school can fill up a whole village!

There are youth hostels at Kirk Yetholm and Wooler. Elsewhere there are inexpensive country inns and B&Bs. And for the truly economical on the high-level route, there is an open shelter at Auchope Cairn, high on the slopes of the Cheviot.

Railway Inn, Newtown St Boswells

There are several campsites along the Way. Discreet and responsible wild camping is a legal right in Scotland. In England it isn't, not even on the access land defined by the *Countryside and Rights of Way Act*.

The Way remains at fairly low altitudes, and there is little if any drinkable water to be found. So refill your water bottle/bladder at every opportunity: most cafés and pubs will oblige a genuine customer. Shops for food supplies are sparse in places. Between St Boswells and Town Yetholm you pass only one shop, the Morebattle Village Shop, which is open only in the mornings: see page 40. There's no food and drink between Kirk Yetholm and Wooler, nor between Wooler and Holy Island.

Templehall Hotel, Morebattle

Travel: times and tides

Table 3 shows recommended journey options and times for travel. To reach Melrose from Edinburgh, use the Borders Railway which opened in 2015. Trains to Tweedbank are frequent, and the final 3km to Melrose can be done by bus or on foot: see page 29 for directions and page 61 for train frequency. You can also reach Melrose from Edinburgh by bus, but there is only one direct coach daily (National Express); First Bus services take longer and require a change.

To reach Melrose from Newcastle and places to its south, the easiest method is a Virgin East Coast train to Berwick (service is fast and frequent), then Perryman's bus to Melrose (departs roughly half hourly). Again, National Express has a direct coach from Newcastle, but only one daily.

Getting away from Lindisfarne is more challenging: the tides dictate when you can reach and leave the island. From Holy Island village, Perryman's local bus 477 reaches Berwick in 35 minutes, but it runs only once or twice a day in season, at times that depend on the tides – and barely at all out of season. It may be more feasible to walk back (or take a taxi) to the mainland, tides permitting, a distance of 5½ miles (9km) through Beal to reach Beal Filling Station (Lindisfarne Service Station) on the A1 trunk road. From here, Arriva runs buses roughly hourly to Berwick, where you join the

Table 3: Distances and journey time to the start and from the finish

from	to	ml	km	means of travel	time (fastest)
Edinburgh (Waverley) ✳	Melrose	40	63	train to Tweedbank	<1hr
Edinburgh bus station ✳	Melrose	40	63	bus	1hr 20min-2 hrs
Newcastle upon Tyne ✳	Melrose via Berwick	100	161	train to Berwick, then bus	2hr 30min
Newcastle upon Tyne ✳	Melrose	72	116	bus (one daily)	2hr
Berwick-upon-Tweed	Melrose	37	60	Perryman's bus	1hr 30min
Beal Filling Station ◆	Berwick-upon-Tweed	10	16	bus	21-25min
Berwick-upon-Tweed	Edinburgh (Waverley)	57	92	train	45-50min
Berwick-upon-Tweed	Newcastle upon Tyne	63	101	train	45-55min
Beal Filling Station ◆	Newcastle upon Tyne	59	95	bus	2hr+

✳ *For travel from the nearest airport, add 35-50 minutes to each time: see text.*
◆ *Travel times from Lindisfarne are longer, but vary with the tides: instead we show times from the bus stops at Beal Filling Station (TD15 2PD).*

railway network. (If heading south, you could instead take an Arriva bus to Alnwick, but far fewer trains stop there.)

For those travelling by air, Edinburgh airport is convenient for reaching Melrose. To reach Edinburgh city centre (for trains and buses) take either the bus or tram: both take about 25-30 minutes for the journey. From Newcastle airport, trains to central Newcastle are fast (25 minutes) and very frequent. (The thrice-daily Line 131 bus from Newcastle to Jedburgh goes via the airport, but including a change of bus at Jedburgh, the journey to Melrose takes 2½-3 hours.)

On Holy Island, Lindisfarne Castle is open only when the causeway is passable. While the castle is open, there's a frequent shuttle bus from the car park at the north end of the village to the castle. But unless you're footsore or strapped for time, you may well prefer to walk the extra 1km.

Holy Island is truly an island for only 4 or 5 hours in every 12. For motorists, there's a causeway which is open when the tide allows. Safe crossing times are found online, see page 60, or by phoning Wooler or Berwick information centres. They are also on a signboard at the causeway's end. The times posted are conservative: strong winds can affect the causeway's opening, and I have seen cars crossing 50 minutes before the advertised time, so it may be worth turning up earlier. However it would be foolish to count on a favourable wind to let you cross *after* the last advertised safe time. In severe storms, the safe crossing period may be *reduced*. If you see water across the causeway, whatever the noticeboard may say, use common sense and turn back.

The RAF helicopter, coastguard and RNLI are efficient at rescuing stranded motorists from the causeway or from the raised rescue shelter at its centre. But they do not rescue cars, which are destroyed by immersion in salt water.

If trapped by the tides, phone 999 and ask the emergency operator for 'coastguard'. Note that rescue is extremely expensive, and the lifeboat is paid for by donations, not by the government. If you have to be rescued, a substantial donation to RNLI is appropriate.

The Way officially crosses by the causeway, which is worth trying to avoid during busy times of day. It's narrow and heavily used, including by coach traffic. It takes about 20 minutes of brisk walking to cover the mile (1·5km) of road causeway.

The Pilgrims' Path is lower lying than the causeway, by up to 2m/7ft. The 'path' stays below high tide level for 2½ mi/4km, so it's passable for a much shorter period than the causeway. The advertised 'safe crossing' times are for the road causeway only. On a falling tide, **wait at least an hour** after the causeway opens before attempting the Pilgrims' Path. And it would be unwise to set out across these sands on a rising tide. Work out when low tide occurs (midway between causeway opening and closing) and set out across the Pilgrims' Path before that time.

> ### Tides at Easter
> The Synod of Whitby was held in AD664: see page 18. It was convened to settle the correct date for Easter, agreed as the first Sunday after the first full moon after 20th March. A neat consequence of the Synod is that Easter pilgrims who arrive at Beal Sands on the morning of Good Friday will always find the tide is out, ready for their crossing of the Pilgrims' Path.

For example, if the safe period for causeway crossing is shown as 12.00 to 21.00, then low tide is halfway between, at about 16.30. The earliest time for the Pilgrims' Path will be about 13.00, and the latest setting-out time would be about 16.30. The tidal sand and soft mud makes for slow going: allow at least 1½ hours.

Towards an emergency refuge on the Pilgrims' Path

Waymarking and navigation

The Way is waymarked at every turn-off junction with the splayed St Cuthbert's Cross or a signpost. Waymarker posts are also placed at many intermediate junctions. Where the route crosses open field or hillside, the path may be narrow, with marker posts at about 200m intervals. These are not always inter-visible if cloud or mist descends, although the recent, black waymarkers are easier to spot from a distance.

The trail is not heavily used – part of its attraction – so it isn't always wide or well-trampled. Read ahead in the route description and study the map for an idea of where you *should* be going. A compass is useful: you don't need sophisticated skills or accurate bearings. If you know you should be heading north-east, and find that you are actually heading south, you can correct your course without wasting too much time or effort.

 Note that North is rotated on all panels of our dropdown map: the North arrow points to the left side of the page, not the top.

Several of our side-trips, are waymarked as the Borders Abbeys Way. These paths are clear and easy to follow – except for the high-level variant over the Cheviot. The upward part of this carries widely-spaced Pennine Way acorn markers, and the descent to Wooler has only occasional yellow arrows marking the right of way. For this adventurous alternative, you need a large-scale map and compass (and perhaps a GPS).

Waymarker below Tom Tallon's Crag

Crookedshaws Hill from Wideopen Hill

Access

Walkers have free access to the whole of the Way throughout the year and at all times of day. The route straddles Scotland and England, and the access situation on the ground beside the path differs in the two countries. In Scotland, walkers have access to almost anywhere, provided that access is taken responsibly. Here is the official short summary of rights in Scotland:

Everyone has the right to be on most land and inland water providing they act responsibly. Your access rights and responsibilities are explained fully in the Scottish Outdoor Access Code.

KNOW THE CODE BEFORE YOU GO
outdooraccess-scotland.com

Whether you're in the outdoors or managing the outdoors, the key things are to
• **take responsibility for your own actions** • **respect the interests of other people** • **care for the environment.**
Find out more by visiting *www.outdooraccess-scotland.com* or by contacting Scottish Natural Heritage; see page 60.

In England, rights of way are marked on Ordnance Survey and other maps. In addition, Access Land is marked on recent maps. However, access to so-called Access Land may be withdrawn or conditional. Restrictions on Access Land are given at *www.openaccess.gov.uk*.

Access with dogs

Much of the Way passes through farmland. There may be cattle or sheep alongside the path. So your dog must be under close control, and preferably on a lead. During lambing time, between April and June, your dog will be unwelcome in any fields with sheep. During the same months, birds are nesting on the ground on moorlands, and again dogs must be under very close control. On much moorland in England, dogs are forbidden for parts of the year, or at all times.

Caution: cows to the left, calves to the right

Be extra careful near cattle when walking with a dog. The photograph above show the Way near Hazelrigg, passing between cows and their calves. Approach cattle with caution – whether walking with or without a dog.

 If cattle react aggressively to your dog, let go of it immediately and take the safest route out of the field. Useful advice on what the *Scottish Outdoor Access Code* means for dog owners is in the free leaflet *Dog Owners* published by Scottish Natural Heritage: see page 60.

Common Ridings

Each year, towns and villages in the Borders celebrate their reiving history with colourful Common Ridings. The festivals last a week (Jedburgh two weeks), culminating with a day of horse ridings. For extra atmosphere, time your walk to coincide with these: see panel. Lovers of peace and quiet may prefer to avoid these dates.

> **Common Ridings and festivals**
> **mid-June:** Melrose Festival Week with ridings based around Melrose Abbey; also Yetholm Summer Festival
> **Sunday in late June:** horseback rideout to Morebattle from both Jedburgh and Kelso: the Jethart Callant meets the Kelso Laddie
> **late June:** Galashiels Braw Lads Gathering
> **late June through to early July:** Jethart Callant's Festival (Jedburgh)
> **last week in July:** Glendale Festival, Wooler (music, crafts, parades)
> **August bank holiday Monday:** Glendale Agricultural Show, Wooler
> *www.returntotheridings.co.uk*

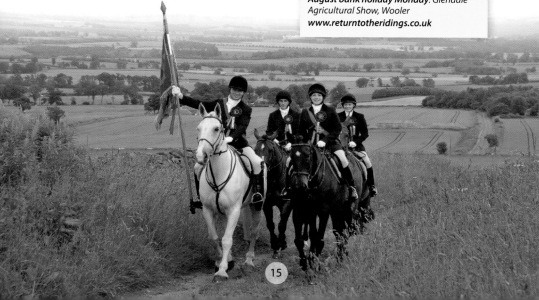

What to bring

Those accustomed to hill and moorland walking will already know what they need. The standard contents of a British walker's rucksack are shown below under 'essential' and should suffice for the Way itself. If you choose the high crossing over the Cheviot, then some items change categories and are *essential*: survival bag, whistle, torch, and large-scale map: see page 60.

Some equipment decisions depend on your choice of accommodation and others on whether you use a baggage transfer service: see page 61. Carrying a tent and other overnight equipment saves money. But then, you'd save even more money by not setting out. Walking the Way should be a pleasure, not an ordeal, and it's more enjoyable without a heavy load. Just pack the essentials for warmth, nourishment and safety.

The Borders is not a wealthy area. Rather than bringing all your needs with you, be prepared to spend some money along the Way. Using local shops and transport helps to keep them viable for local people as well.

Cash machines are at Melrose, Wooler and Jedburgh. Small supermarkets, some B&Bs and post offices offer 'cashback' – a cash withdrawal in addition to a purchase made with your credit or debit card. Many B&Bs do not accept credit/debit cards and a cheque book may be useful. Mobile phone reception is fairly good over most parts of the walk, on most networks.

A mobile phone is desirable if taking the Pilgrims' Path: see page 57. A 999 call will be connected via any available network.

Packing checklist

Essential

• rucksack (30 litres minimum)
• waterproof rucksack cover, or liner, or plastic bags
• walking boots, lightweight if possible
• plenty of walking socks, fairly new
• breathable shirt, trousers
• fleece top
• spare clothing for when daywear soaked
• waterproof jacket and overtrousers
• gloves and warm hat
• midge repellent (midge net if camping)
• compass
• guidebook
• water bottle (1 litre minimum)
• food including small emergency ration
• first aid kit
• cash, credit/debit card

Desirable/useful

• poles
• survival bag/space blanket
• whistle and torch
• GPS
• gaiters
• slippers/trainers for overnight
• camera and spares (batteries, cards, film)
• binoculars for birdlife
• notebook/diary and pen
• rucksack pockets/bumbag for small items
• mobile phone
• sun cream, sun hat

2·1 The striding saints

During the Dark Ages, starting from various offshore islands, Christianity spread inwards across Britain in small boats and on foot. The Celtic saints were the long-distance walkers of their times. People lived in tribal villages from which it was dangerous to stray into the next glen, but the saints strode from one side of the country to the other – obeying their Master's command to 'take the Gospel to the ends of the Earth'. From St Patrick's settlement at Iona, St Aidan walked diagonally coast to coast to establish his own foundation at Lindisfarne. Aidan was presented with a horse by the Christian King Oswald of Northumbria. As soon as possible, Aidan passed it on to a poor man who, in his opinion, needed it more.

This made sense in practical terms. In unsettled tribal lands, a saint on foot – with no possessions and possibly not even carrying food – would scarcely be worth the trouble of murdering. But also, Aidan just loved long journeys on foot. His successor St Chad was similarly embarrassed by a gift horse, and managed to get rid of it.

Cuthbert, the third Prior of Lindisfarne, was born in AD634 and probably grew up as a shepherd in the Cheviot fringes, or possibly on the Eildons themselves. At the age of 16 he had a vision of St Aidan being carried into Heaven by angels. He embraced the religious life, and became a novice monk at Old Melrose. Within ten years he was its prior. Old Melrose was a few miles east of the present Melrose, in a bend of the Tweed, but almost nothing remains of it today.

Statue of St Cuthbert, Lindisfarne Priory

Old Melrose was a substation of Lindisfarne, founded by St Aidan in AD635 and staffed with monks from Iona. A few years later, Cuthbert's abbot, Eata, was appointed Bishop of Lindisfarne, and he took his capable young prior Cuthbert along with him. So St Cuthbert's Way celebrates Cuthbert's life journey from Melrose to Lindisfarne. But for Cuthbert and his colleagues, 62 miles would have been little more than a weekend break.

There must have been much monkish walking back and forth between the two foundations, along the old Roman road through the Cheviots and across Glendale.

Cuthbert also walked much further afield. His missionary journeys probably took him to Iona, and he is recorded in Glen Lyon in central Perthshire. Under Hadrian's Wall near Housesteads is Cuddy's Crag, where he probably preached – Cuddy being his Northumbrian nickname. Every year he walked across England to visit his friend St Herbert, who lived on an island in Derwent Water. His colleagues from Lindisfarne are recorded journeying far north into Scotland as well as south to East Anglia and even Tilbury.

At the Synod of Whitby, the crucial church conference of AD664, England adopted the Roman rather than the Celtic version of Christianity. Cuthbert was there as a conciliator, and in the following years he helped the Celtic style to be absorbed into the Roman one within the Lindisfarne monastery.

In AD676, aged 42, Cuthbert retired early to become a hermit on the Farne Islands. He built himself a small cell, where he prayed and slept. He hacked a well out of bedrock, and scraped together enough soil to grow barley.

What stands today as Cuthbert's Chapel dates from about 1300 and was restored in the mid-19th century, using woodwork brought from Durham Cathedral. The stained glass windows show Cuthbert as bishop (left) and hermit (right).

In AD 684, at the age of 50, Cuthbert was summoned back to Lindisfarne to become its bishop. Within three years, his health had broken and he was carried back to his beloved Inner Farne to die. Under his brief, Lindisfarne became the library of the church. Scrolls were inscribed on vellum (specially prepared calfskin). Holy Island had its own vellum factory with two workshops, a slaughterhouse and a midden with the bones of scores of calves. Hundreds of books were hand-written and crafted here.

Immediately after his death in AD687, the famous Lindisfarne Gospels were inscribed in Cuthbert's memory. Their 258 pages consumed 130 calfskins, and involved two man-years of work just for the illustrations. The book's decorations included blue lapis lazuli imported from the foothills of the Himalaya.

In AD698, Cuthbert was dug up and found to be miraculously preserved. In later years, Cuthbert's corpse continued his long-distance travels. Following the first Viking raid on Lindisfarne in AD793, Cuthbert and the Lindisfarne Gospels were carried westwards for safety. On its way to Workington his body rested at Cuthbert's Cave: see page 54.

Meanwhile, the Lindisfarne Gospels *en route* to Ireland were lost in a shipwreck on the Irish Sea. Cuthbert appeared in a vision and told the monks where to find it again, washed up on the shore. Seawater stains on the gospel, now held at the British Library, corroborate this story.

Later, Cuthbert's corpse reached Ripon, but because of marauding Danes, in AD995 it was moved again to Durham. Here a church was built above his new grave. In 1104 his remains were transferred to a shrine in the newly completed Durham Cathedral. This became a popular place of pilgrimage throughout the Middle Ages.

During the Reformation, Cuthbert's shrine was dismantled but the monks managed to hide his remains. In 1827 Cuthbert's coffin, still containing his bones, was dug up and opened. Around his neck was his beautiful pectoral (chest-worn) cross, made of gold and studded with garnets. His original (AD698) coffin and this cross are on display at Durham Cathedral. A stylised version of the four-armed Cuthbert Cross is used today as the logo of St Cuthbert's Way.

The Cuthbert Cross, Durham Cathedral

2·2 History

Hill forts and Roman roads

Long before St Aidan founded Melrose Abbey, the Eildons were a long-distance path junction. The largest hill fort in Scotland lies beneath the bilberry and heather of Eildon Hill North. This Bronze Age and Iron Age settlement, with its 5km of ramparts, was the capital of the tribe the Romans referred to as the *Selgovae*.

Roman era grindstone

The steep-sided foothills of the Cheviots provided many more settlements. Covered in short, sheep-cropped grass, these are easier for the non-archeologist to spot. Seven are passed along St Cuthbert's Way, the most spectacular being on Yeavering Bell, where fallen stonework circles the hilltop: see page 44. These Cheviot forts were mainly places of retreat during enemy raids. The one on Eildon was also a permanent settlement, with the remains of 300 hut circles. The huts were of wickerwork and mud, thatched with heather. The people made beautiful pottery, as well as bronze swords and knives. They wore woven woollen cloaks, tunics and hats.

The Romans in turn adopted Eildon as a communications centre. At the foot of the eastern slope they built their large fort of *Trimontium*, or 'Triple Mountain'. The fort was a large one, with a bath house and an inn for travellers. On Eildon Hill North they built a signal station. Its first use may have been as a survey point for Dere Street, the Roman road across the plains from the south.

Fort on Eildon Hill North

In use ever since, Dere Street is the line of several miles of St Cuthbert's Way. Its ruler-like straightness is an obvious clue to its origins, even though no Roman remains are visible on the ground. However, you can see such remains in the museum alongside Melrose Abbey, and also at the Three Hills Roman Heritage Centre in Melrose's Market Square.

As a shepherd, Cuthbert was part of a thriving local wool industry – and as prior of Melrose, he remained so. Monks were the entrepreneurs of the Middle Ages, with prosperous abbeys across the Borders: Melrose, Dryburgh, Jedburgh and Kelso.

As the feudal system developed into the nation state, the border abbeys were in the front line between Scotland and its expansionist neighbour England. Melrose Abbey was destroyed and rebuilt several times. Its final

Dere Street south-east of Jedfoot Bridge

destruction was in 1544. Henry VIII wanted to unite the kingdoms under himself by marrying the infant Mary Queen of Scots to his son Prince Edward. In what was called the 'Rough Wooing', he sent the Earl of Hertford to persuade the princess by burning down all four of the border abbeys along with the surrounding countryside.

Dryburgh Abbey from the south

The raid culminated in a battle on Ancrum Moor in 1545. The English were outmanoeuvred and defeated. Notable in the battle was a local woman called Lilliard, who took up arms to avenge her lover, killed by the English.

The site was supposedly renamed Lilliard's Edge in her honour. However this placename was recorded before the battle ever happened, and the stump-thumping is derived from the 'Ballad of Chevy Chase', a battle of 150 years earlier.

Upon the English loons
She laid monie thumps
An when her legs were cuttit off
She fought upon her stumps.

['loons' = lads, 'monie' = many]

Reivers and raiders

The Border Wars weren't the worst of it. The two monarchs chose to leave the Borders as a buffer zone between England and Scotland. What was convenient for Edinburgh and London was lethal for those who lived here. For 200 years, no law ran in the Borders but blood-feud and counter-raid. Survival depended on alliance with a powerful local warlord, such as Kerr of Cessford Castle.

The Kerrs (or Kers or Carrs) were a tribe raiding on either side of the border. Come the autumn full moon, a farmer might find the Kerrs (or Elliots, Armstrongs or Nixons) descending, his house burnt, his cattle driven away across the hills, and his family left to starve slowly over the coming winter. The author's own ancestors, cattle raiders out of Teviotdale, were once at deadly feud with the Kerrs of Cessford.

With the Union of the crowns of England and Scotland in 1603, law gradually returned to the Borders. The Kerrs became the respectable Earls of Roxburgh. But the legacy of those terrible times remains, and not just in the raucous, horseback 'Common Riding' ceremonies of Jedburgh and other Border towns, not only in their tradition of seven-a-side Rugby. The scattered population of the Cheviot dales, their eerie silence below the skylarks and the keening wind, can be traced back to the raids and starvation of reiving times.

Cessford Castle

2·3 Land and wildlife

The Way passes through five distinct habitats, described below from west to east:

The Eildons   **River Tweed**   **Farmland**   **Moor and mountain**   **Coast**

The Eildons

The Eildons stick up almost like volcanoes from their surroundings. Indeed, their rocks were the foundations of volcanoes that erupted here about 300 million years ago. However, their conical shapes are not volcanic, but due to their red trachyte rock being harder and resisting erosion more than the surrounding sandstones. The stonework of Melrose is a mixture of this volcanic rock with the yellowish-brown sandstone of the Tweed valley, giving a pleasing mottled effect.

The hills themselves are clothed in heather, bilberry, and gorse. This reflects their impoverished, rubbly soil, from which nutrients easily drain away. It also reflects past overgrazing by sheep. Over nearly all of the Southern Uplands, the natural vegetation would be wild woodland of birch and oak. Those trees have been cleared, over centuries, by people and by sheep. Today, upland sheep farming is becoming uneconomic, and these hills are under protection as the Eildon and Leaderfoot National Scenic Area. The natural treeline is moving steadily uphill.

Stonework of Melrose Abbey museum
Below: basalt quarry at col of the Eildons

23

Buzzard feeding on rabbit

Walkers can still enjoy outstanding views from these hilltops, and are likely to spot buzzards soaring in the updraughts above the steep slopes, mewing like lost kittens. By late summer, a family of half a dozen buzzards may be spiralling in the same upward air current.

River Tweed

The Way meets the Tweed at St Boswells. Here it is neither a young river with deeply-carved channel, rock bed and waterfalls; nor a mature river, winding across a wide flood plain. It seems more teen-aged – full-sized and strong, impetuous in its flow. It has in fact 60m still to fall (and 70km of distance to flow) before it reaches the sea at Berwick.

The story of the river is the same as of the land: two centuries of damage by man, now turned around and slowly being restored. The Tweed Foundation has been fencing the banks of Tweed and its tributaries, allowing tree growth, and insects which fall into the river to feed trout and young salmon. The ecology repairs are succeeding. In recent years, the Tweed has been the top salmon river in the entire European Union in terms of the number of fish caught.

The river is home to many ducks, from the common mallard to the rare fish-eating goosander, now breeding here. It is longer and thinner than a mallard, with a saw-tooth beak.

Herons are abundant, seen at intervals along the river. Other fish predators include mammals such as otter and mink.

Mature salmon work their way up river, reaching the Teviot in late summer, St Boswells a month or so later. After heavy rain with the rivers in spate, they may be spotted leaping up the *cauls* (artificial weirs) at Melrose, upstream from Mertoun Bridge, and on the Teviot at Monteviot.

Long green fronds and white buttercup-type flowers of water crowfoot stream in the river. On the Tweed's banks at the back of Newtown St Boswells, the rich volcanic basalt soils give a jungle growth of ash trees and rhubarb-like *Gunnera*. The spectacular giant hogweed also survives here and there along the riverside. Because it causes an allergic skin reaction, it's heavily persecuted by local authorities.

Heron on River Tweed

Water crowfoot below the green footbridge of the Tweed

Oilseed rape below St Cuthbert's Cave

Farmland

Between the Tweed and the Cheviots, the Way passes through pastureland, grazed by cattle and sheep. The rich soils are coloured by the underlying Old Red Sandstone, which formed from sand and silt washed out of an Alp-sized mountain range 400 million years ago. The red debris layered itself across the floor of a shallow sea. At the footbridge of Oxnam Water, the stream has exposed a 20m-high cliff. The sediments built up layer by layer suggest the huge time-span taken to form them. Such sites helped the geologists of the Scottish Enlightenment in the early 19th century to reject the Bible's creation story.

You may well spot a brown hare dashing across the pastureland or startle one standing on the road. Other wildlife is found in the field edges, with dog rose lovely in June, and many small birds thriving in the hedges. Woodlands scattered among the fields harbour roe deer, as well as squirrels both grey and red. Throughout the Borders, grey squirrels are inexorably supplanting the native reds.

After Wooler you pass through lower, more fertile farmland, where the rabbit replaces the hare and oilseed rape colours the fields vivid yellow.

Brown hare

Yellowhammer on gorse

Moor and mountain

The foothills on the Scottish side of the Cheviots are small, steep-sided and grassy – just asking to be walked over. And between Morebattle and Wooler, St Cuthbert's Way strides along the 300m contour.

At a wall on Gains Law, the track passes from grassy moorland to heather. The abrupt change at the boundary wall confirms that its cause is land management. Exclusion of hungry sheep has preserved heather moorland – the UK's own special ecosystem. Its notable residents are the red grouse, which depends totally on heather both for food and nest sites, and some heather-adapted caterpillars. In July, the bell heather and cross-leaved heath flower in small clumps on rocky outcrops. A month later, it's the ling, with tiny leaves and flowers, that floats its purple haze across the moorland.

Bedstraw, tormentil and milkwort

By contrast, grass moorland in June offers a tapestry of small bright wildflowers: white bedstraw, yellow tormentil, and tiny blue flowers of milkwort. Overhead, the sky is full of the sound of skylarks. A small brown bird with two white flashes in the tail is the meadow pipit. The wheatear is another small brown bird, but with a single white flash on its rump – its name derives from 'white-arse'.

Heather moorland, home to red grouse (inset)

Oystercatcher

Coast

The coastal end of the walk is its climax. Here is a very different sort of scenery, symbolised by the crabs met on the 4km Pilgrims' Path crossing. The mudflats, salt marshes, and dunes of Holy Island are a national nature reserve, which naturalists will want to study in advance. Fragments of fossil sea-lilies (crinoids) found on the foreshore are known as St Cuthbert's beads.

Most walkers will miss the winter waterfowl, which include Brent geese, widgeons, and bar-tailed godwits. Walkers who cross and return during a single low tide will only glimpse the oystercatchers, terns, and seals – both common and grey. For good sightings of all these, as well as gannets, puffins, and eider ducks, stop over and experience the place as a true island, with the sea lapping at its shoreline.

St Cuthbert's Way is completed here. But a tempting postscript is the boat trip from Seahouses to the offshore Farne Islands. The islands are the absolute end-point of the Great Whin Sill (the volcanic rock which crosses northern England). From May to July there is an amazing display of seabirds, nesting just beside the designated pathway. Moreover, it

Eider duck: see below

was Cuthbert's chosen final resting place. On the Farne Islands he built his hermitage retreat, surrounded by sea-spray and the haunting cry of the 'Cuddy Duck', the eider duck whose Northumberland nickname recalls the saint himself.

Tweedbank to Melrose

From Tweedbank station, Melrose is a 7-minute bus ride, with at least three buses per hour. Rather than wait, consider instead this pleasant 3km riverside walk to Melrose, shown on our online route map: see page 60.

- Beyond the station, go straight ahead along a tarmac cycleway with blue sign 'Melrose 1¾ miles'. After 500m, bear left at the green Southern Upland Way sign and descend to the B6374 road.

- Cross to its far side, where a timber fingerpost points right, through a timber gate. Head downhill on the narrow path, muddy in places, past an information board for Skirmish Hill (1526). Descend to the lovely river bank: see pages 24-5 for more about the Tweed.

- Continue downstream on an undulating path, briefly leaving the bank at a timber waymarker (thistle in hexagon) to pass through a kissing-gate. The route joins a road fleetingly, then descends a flight of steps.

- At a timber fingerpost, the SU Way continues ahead to the Chain Bridge. Instead, turn right, signed for Melrose town centre, with a blue E2 disc. Follow the tarmac path past Melrose Parish Church to a crossroads.

- Turn left along the High Street to reach the town centre. Bear left along Buccleuch Street to meet Abbey Street, then turn left for the entrance to Melrose Abbey.

Abbotsford House

Abbotsford House was built by the writer Sir Walter Scott (1771-1832) as a family home, and to display his valuable collection of books, artefacts and weaponry. His Waverley books were, for nearly a century, Europe's most popular novels. His study and library still have his writing desk and books exactly as he worked from them.

Reopened in 2013 after major refurbishment, the house and gardens welcome visitors from March to November (open 10.00-16.00, in season until 17.00). The visitor centre (admission free) and restaurant are open year-round: see *www.scottsabbotsford.com*. Abbotsford is about a mile from Tweedbank station, served by bus. Walking options are documented here: *www.rucsacs.com/books/scw*.

Bust of Walter Scott, Abbotsford House (library)

Melrose

The Way starts at Melrose, near to where St Cuthbert himself started his religious life, becoming its prior around AD660: see page 17. Melrose Abbey was destroyed by Edward II in 1322, and rebuilt by King Robert the Bruce, whose embalmed heart is buried beside the abbey. In 1385 the abbey was burned again by Richard II. But the final destruction was in the 'Rough Wooing' of 1544: see page 21.

Marker for Robert the Bruce's buried heart

Melrose Abbey (below) can be appreciated from the surrounding streets. But it's worth paying the small entry charge: enjoy its interior, ascend the staircase to the viewpoint on top of its walls, and visit its small museum. The abbey is open daily, cared for by Historic Environment Scotland: see page 61 for opening hours.

After the Middle Ages, the focus of Melrose shifted from religion to commerce. The cross that once stood at the entrance to the Abbey precinct also shifted and became the town's Mercat Cross. Almost all of the original cross has been replaced: the oldest part we see is its octagonal base, built only 150 years ago. The rest dates from various times in the last century – with one exception, the metal staple. Petty criminals were tethered to the cross by an iron neck-chain (called the *jougs*) attached to this staple.

The Roman Heritage Museum is also in the town's Mercat Square. It's open daily from April to October between 10.30 to 16.30 (closed Sunday mornings): see *www.trimontium.org.uk*.

3·1 Melrose to Jedfoot Bridge

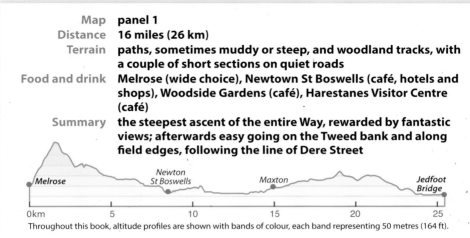

Map	**panel 1**
Distance	**16 miles (26 km)**
Terrain	**paths, sometimes muddy or steep, and woodland tracks, with a couple of short sections on quiet roads**
Food and drink	**Melrose (wide choice), Newtown St Boswells (café, hotels and shops), Woodside Gardens (café), Harestanes Visitor Centre (café)**
Summary	**the steepest ascent of the entire Way, rewarded by fantastic views; afterwards easy going on the Tweed bank and along field edges, following the line of Dere Street**

Throughout this book, altitude profiles are shown with bands of colour, each band representing 50 metres (164 ft).

- From the abbey entrance head south up Abbey Street, with the high wall of Priorwood Gardens on your left. Go straight across Market Square into Dingleton Road, following signs for St Cuthbert Way and Eildon Walk.

- Pass up under the bypass, and after 100m turn off left down steps. A path heads up 133 wooden steps in a wood, then uphill between fields, onto open hill.

- The path slants to the right, around Eildon North, and up to the col to its right – the gap between Eildon North and Eildon Mid Hill. Here you could divert to Eildon Mid Hill – see panel.

- Head down south between the hills on a wide path into woods, soon reaching a track junction. Bear right, briefly level then gently downhill (roughly south).

Eildon Mid Hill from Eildon Hill North

> **Eildon Hills**
>
> *For all-around views stretching from the Southern Uplands (to north and west) to the Cheviots (in the south), ascend one of the Eildon summits. Eildon Hill North is up to your left, though little if anything is visible of its earthworks under the heather and bilberry cover.*
>
> *To reach the main summit, Eildon Mid Hill, take either of the two paths up to the right, afterwards returning to the same point. Or you can head down a small, steep path due south onto Eildon Wester Hill, then descend south-west on another steep path to a stile. Across this, turn left, down alongside a wood and then just inside it. Rejoin the Way at a path junction: see p32, 2nd bullet.*

- The track bends uphill, and below you see the wood foot; here look out for a path forking down left. The path runs downhill just inside the wood, with open fields to the left.

- At the wood's bottom edge, don't join the smooth field track just below. Instead turn right for 400m. At a path junction, turn left, and cross the vehicle track below, into a stand of Scots pines.

- The path heads up steps under the pines for 100m. It continues gently downhill (south), to reach Bowden's main street at the village well.

- Turn right then at once down left, signed for Bowden Kirk. After 100m, the road bends right: instead turn left along a path.

Village well, Bowden

- The path runs down to cross a stream before heading up right to join a track. This runs east above the stream to a road corner.

- Keep ahead along this road (east) past Whitelee. After 1km the road goes under an old railway and over a stream, to reach the main road in Newtown St Boswells. (Turn left up this road to reach the village shops, pub, café and toilets, or turn right for its only B&B.)

- To continue the Way, cross the main road diagonally right into a lane that dips then rises to a red stone shed.

- Turn half left into a lane with a green sign 'Path to river'. The lane twists down towards the A68 flyover.

Bowden from the south

- Just before the flyover, look out for a path forking off right into scrubby woodland, soon crossing a footbridge over a stream. Keep ahead (east) through the woods, then continue up steps to a high river bank overlooking the Tweed.

- The path heads down-river, descending to cross a lane with a green suspension bridge to the left. (To divert to Dryburgh Abbey, cross this bridge: see panel.)

- Keep ahead on a track for 100m, then bear right on a path that remains close to the Tweed, with steps and railings as the bank steepens. After a footbridge the path bends up right to the edge of St Boswells, where you turn left (along Hamilton Place) to the village green.

- Turn left at the green, keeping ahead at its corner to pass shops. In 300m turn left into Braeheads Road.

- Follow the street round to the right, to its end, where you turn down left. Just as you reach the edge of a golf course, look out for a path turnoff to the right. This runs alongside the golf course and eventually reaches the River Tweed.

Dryburgh Abbey

> **_i_ Dryburgh Abbey**
>
> *Peaceful among its trees, Dryburgh Abbey has a special atmosphere. It's invisible from the south bank, and to visit it you must cross the Tweed by suspension bridge (and pay an entry charge). Across the river, follow the lane downstream to a junction. Keep ahead to the car park at the Abbey entrance. It's open daily: for hours, see page 61.*
>
> *To return to the Way, either retrace your steps, or follow the Borders Abbeys Way (north of the Tweed) as far as Mertoun Bridge, and cross it to rejoin the Way: see map.*

Tweed opposite St Boswells golf course

Mertoun Bridge

- The path follows the river, rising up steps to cross the B6404 road at Mertoun Bridge, then descending to continue along the riverside. After another 1km it passes below Crystal Well, an antique water-pumping station for the house above.

- Just afterwards, the path bears right up 62 steps and continues along the bank top overlooking the Tweed. Then it descends by more steps into a wood with wild garlic. After crossing a track, the path rises again up an earth bank.

- The path passes Maxton Kirk to reach a lane. Turn right and follow this to Maxton.

- In Maxton, turn right along the A699 road for 300m, then left into a lane signposted 'Long Newtown'. The lane crosses an old railway then bends right. After 400m, look for a tarred driveway on the left which provides an alternative to the Way.

- We recommend you turn off left along this driveway, which soon bends right to pass Morridgehall Farm and bungalow. At its end, keep ahead on an earth path under tall trees. After 800m, just before the A68, rejoin the official Way by turning left along a track which follows the line of Dere Street, the old Roman road.

- Meanwhile the official Way keeps on along the lane until just before the busy A68, where it turns left on an earth path under trees near the main road.

- The Way runs along the right-hand edge of a field, then again in trees, to reach a grass track along Dere Street, waymarked with a Roman helmet logo.

- This track becomes a field edge path that runs south-east for the next 5km.

Eildons from near Morridgehall

- After the first 1·5km the field-edge path passes a stile on the right leading to the wall-enclosed Lilliard Stone: see page 22.

- After a further 2·5km the path reaches a lane: cross over and continue ahead.

- After 800m, the path crosses a stream and then turns slightly right (south). (After the next footbridge, you could divert up a signed side-path on the right which leads within 100m to Woodside Gardens, with its café.)

- At the next lane, cross to a small gate. (The next side-path on the right leads to a roofed shelter.) Keep ahead across a footbridge: the Way turns left at a signpost.

- To divert to the Harestanes Visitor Centre and café, instead turn right and follow this wide path for 150m, then look out for multicoloured waymarks and a small path forking down to the right. It joins a tarred lane leading to Harestanes.

- The main Way continues through the woods, emerging to cross the driveway of Monteviot House. If time, consider diverting to visit its gardens: see panel. The Way continues along the driveway in a left-right dogleg then through the woods beyond.

- The woodland path swings right and emerges into a field, where it heads directly downhill into trees beside River Teviot. The path bends right to a suspension bridge.

- Cross the river and turn left, downstream. After 1km the path bends right and follows the River Jed upstream, before ascending to a crash barrier beside Jedfoot Bridge.

- Turn left across the A698 road bridge, then right into a lane. After 100m turn left up a stony track. (To divert to Jedburgh, ignore the track and keep ahead on the lane: see page 36).

> *i* **Monteviot House and gardens**
> Monteviot House is home to Lord Lothian, a descendent of the Kerr cattle-reiving family. The elegant sandstone house is Georgian, with later additions. Its 'eccentric and tangled' interior has fine plaster ceilings and family portraits. Open to the public only on July afternoons (not Mondays). The gardens are open daily 12.00 to 17.00, April to October. The design makes the most of its superb location within a curve of the River Teviot. A laburnum tunnel leads to a water garden created from a spring-fed bog. House and gardens make a small entry charge, see **www.monteviot.com**.

Jedburgh

- From Jedfoot Bridge the lane leads south for 3km, to join A68 at the edge of Jedburgh. 'Borders Abbeys Way' waymarks now lead on into Jedburgh.

- With a bridge over River Jed on your right, cross the main A68 road to the tarmac Waterside Walk. Follow it upstream, with the river on your right, for 1km.

- Keep ahead on back streets, then cross an old road bridge over the river. Bend round left to join High Street to Jedburgh Abbey. It's open daily, cared for by Historic Environment Scotland: see page 61 for opening hours.

- You can leave Jedburgh by a short-cut on a pleasant path, waymarked Borders Abbeys Way. Start by retracing steps along Waterside Walk, across A68, and back up the small lane.

- After the lane's first steep climb under trees, ignore a first side-road on the right, but in another 300m, fork right to pass Woodend Farm (a cottage). The lane rises past a radio mast.

- Where the lane bends right at a house, wiggle left to a field top path. Beyond the house, join a smooth hedged path for 1km to the T-junction where the Borders Abbeys Way meets St Cuthbert's: turn up right and follow directions from the second bullet on page 38.

Jedburgh has much to offer the visitor. There's the 12th-century Augustinian Abbey, still impressive in ruins. Mary Queen of Scots' House is a handsome stone building, formerly thatched, containing furnishings, tapestry and armour from the 16th century. Mary fell dangerously ill with a fever here in 1566; later, in her long captivity in England, she wished: 'Would that I had died in Jedburgh'.

At the south end of the town you can sample Victorian prison life at the Castle Jail. And throughout the handsome town centre you enjoy its free WiFi access.

Only 10 miles from the English Border, in the lawless Scottish Middle March, Jedburgh was at the heart of the raids and skirmishes of the reiving times (see page 22). The town held its own among the local warlords, forming an alliance with Kerr of Cessford (see page 40) against the rival Kerrs of Ferniehurst. For many years, indeed, the town and the Kerrs of Ferniehurst were formally at feud.

During one local war in 1572 a messenger arrived at the town with messages from Mary Queen of Scots; the town was loyal to her infant son, King James VI, and made the messenger eat his own message. The town had its own, much-feared, battle cry: "Jethart's here!" Jethart justice consisted of hanging a man first and trying him afterwards: the Jethart staff was a long-handled battle-axe for use on horseback.

More innocently, Jethart Snails are a brown boiled sweet supposedly introduced to the town by prisoners from Napoleon's army. But the town's robust heritage lingers on in the Jethart Hand Ba', a version of medieval football played every February with half the town in each team, based around the Mercat Cross. Above all is the two-week long Callant's Festival, the town's common-riding that starts on the last Saturday in June.

Jedburgh High Street

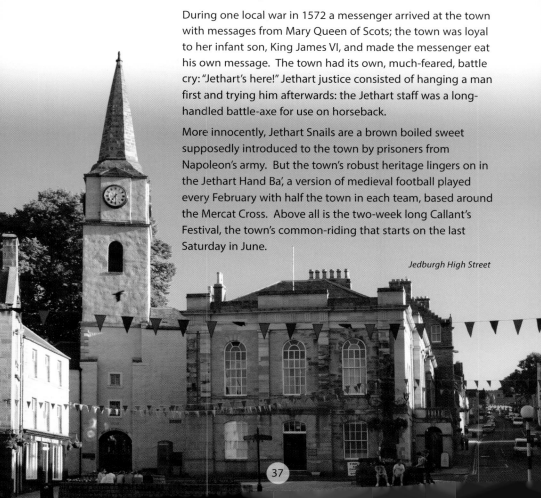

3·2 Jedfoot Bridge to Kirk Yetholm

Map	**panel 2**
Distance	**15 miles (24 km)**
Terrain	**paths through fields and woods, followed by a small grass path over low hills**
Food and drink	**Morebattle (shop, hotel), Town Yetholm (shops, hotels), Kirk Yetholm (hotel)**
Summary	**high pastureland alternating with small woods for the first half; after Morebattle, grassy Wideopen Hill**

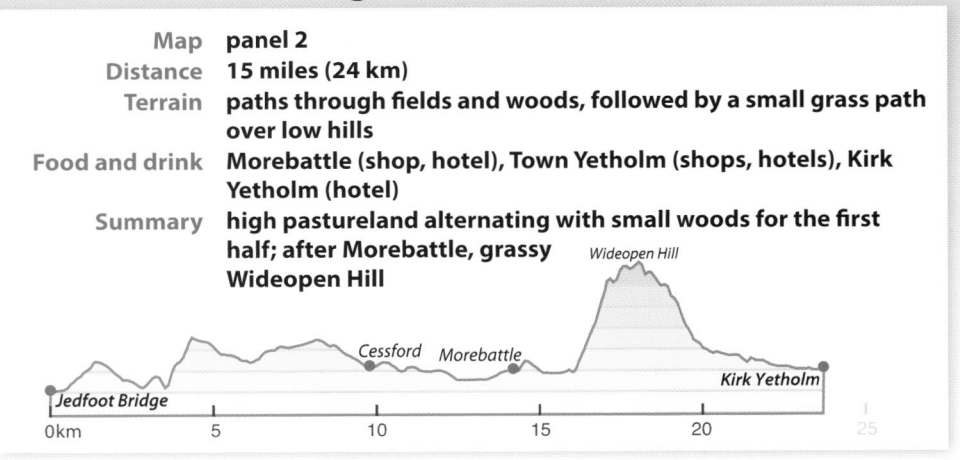

- From the turnoff just after Jedfoot Bridge, follow the track quite steeply uphill, to where a side-path on the right is signposted to Jedburgh by the Borders Abbeys Way.

- From the path junction, keep uphill on the stony track of St Cuthbert's Way for 200m. Turn left at a horse stile into a strip of woodland, and follow the small green path for one mile (1·5km) to a lane.

- Turn right for 300m to where the lane bends right. Here bear left into a green track, leading down to Oxnam Water, which you cross by a footbridge on the right. Just upstream is a fine outcrop of Old Red Sandstone: see picture below and page 26.

- After the footbridge, turn half-left (south-east) across the riverside field and up through a gate. As the slope eases a bit, the faint path bends left (north) to reach trees, then bends back right to a gate to the right of a house.

- Follow the tarmac driveway track away from the house, steeply uphill. At its top turn left through more woodland.

- The path heads north under tall beeches, to reach another lane. Turn right for 400m to a T-junction. Turn left for 40m, then go through a kissing-gate on the right just before Brownrigg House.

i **Waterloo Monument**
The Tweed valley is dotted with small hills that proved inviting to builders of monuments and follies. Most prominent of these is the 150ft-high Waterloo Monument on Peniel Heugh. The first attempt at a monument, a massive stone pyramid, stood less than a year before collapsing 'with a tremendous crash'. Its replacement, a column with spiral staircase, was completed in 1824. From its viewing platform you can survey many miles of St Cuthbert's Way, and it's a popular picnic spot. If you've time to spare, the climb takes you only about a mile off-route from Monteviot: refer to a large-scale map.

- Head down to cross a footbridge, then skirt around the foot of a field. This leaves you heading uphill (south) to bear left on a track into some trees. This is the first of three woodlands in this section.

- Follow the track down into a dip. As it rises again, it narrows to a path which runs along the left edge of the woodland to a gate at its corner.

- The path continues along the right edge of a field, then the right edge of the second wood, which is of pines. Keep straight on along the right edge of another field, to bend left (north-east) at its corner.

- Turn right over a wall stile to head slightly uphill, with a wall on your right, to the third wood, a hilltop plantation.

- Turn left alongside the wood, then turn right around its corner and along its northern edge. At a track junction, turn left, away from the wood.

Waterloo Monument from Mount Ulston path

Cessford Castle

- Over the next 2km the track runs downhill, north-east then east, to Cessford. Bear right over a stream to Cessford Farm, where you turn left.

- The road leads toward and past Cessford Castle: see panel.

- After the castle, descend to the B6401. Here you turn right past the wall of Otterburn House and into Morebattle.

Morebattle's name has nothing to do with fighting, but means 'marsh settlement' from the swamp or mere, Linton Loch, that once lay just to its north. Morebattle Village Shop is open mornings only (from 7.00-13.00 on weekdays, with shorter opening at weekends). There is also the Templehall Hotel, an inn at the eastern end of the village: see page 9.

- At the east end of Morebattle, bear right up a lane signed Hownam. After 1km it drops to meet a road, where you turn right.

- Follow the road for 500m and turn left to cross the Kale Water by a footbridge. Cross a field to join a track, and turn right on this.

- The track passes up to right of an old quarry, then zigzags uphill to a point behind a small hill fort. Turn right over a ladder stile and head uphill to the right of a plantation.

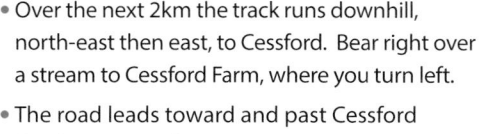

Cessford Castle

Interpretation boards present the uncertain and uncomfortable life of the fortress in the reiving times: see page 22. Cessford was the stronghold of a branch of the Kerr family. Kerr was 'Carr' on the English side of the border, but the same warrior tribe, and equally feared in both countries. Robert Kerr of Cessford was the most notorious raider, blackmailer and feuder of the late 16th century.

According to legend, many of the Kerrs were left-handed. While most such refuge towers had a spiral staircase favouring the right arm of the swordsman retreating upwards, the Kerr strongholds had their staircases spiralling the other way, anticlockwise. Because of the dangerous stonework, it's not possible to verify this.

- The path heads uphill through grass, to pass just left of the first hump, Grubbit Law.

- In the next col, ignore a crossing track, and bend left (north-east) to join a wall. The path follows the main ridge line with the wall on its left, to cross a ladder stile on the second summit hump.

- The path and wall continue to the third summit, Wideopen Hill: see panel.

- Now the ridge wall bends right, downhill, before bending back left, through another slight col. Bypass a basalt outcrop before continuing gently down the ridgeline, always keeping the wall to your left, as waymarked. In mist, maintain the direction north-east as you descend.

i **Wideopen Hill**

At 367m (1208ft) this is the highest point of the Way (although not yet its half-way point). Rising steeply at the northern edge of the Cheviot range, it offers views over the wide plains of the Tweed. Back in the west is the Waterloo Monument, with the triple top of Eildon beyond, 16 miles away as the crow flies. Below you, in the same direction, low sunlight may reveal the Iron Age settlement on Morebattle Hill.

To the north-east, the ridge points along Bowmont Water to Kirk Yetholm. Just to the left, behind Yetholm Law, gleams the water of Yetholm Loch. Southwards the views are shorter, rising to the ridgeline of the Cheviots with the English border along the skyline. At its left end rises the wide hump of the Cheviot itself, decorated by tiny granite tors.

- As the descending ridge reaches fields, the path turns right over a ladder stile, then after 50m back down the ridgeline over another stile.

- Pass through the clump of trees (shown below) to reach a further stile into a lane. Turn right, down to a road beside Bowmont Water.

- Turn left for 1·5km to Primsidemill. Join the B6401 towards Town Yetholm.

- After 500m, beside a cemetery, turn off right into a minor road. Within 60m turn left on a green track to the riverside. Cross a field to a road bridge between the Yetholms. (This bridge is the half-way point of the Way, and not Wideopen Hill as its sign claims.)

- Turn right across the bridge, and take a path on the opposite side of the road. It crosses one field, then bends right into Kirk Yetholm.

Clump of trees on the descent from Wideopen Hill

3·3a Kirk Yetholm to Wooler

Map	**panels 2 and 3**
Distance	**13 miles (21 km)**
Terrain	**moorland paths and tracks, with one indistinct section (leaving Hethpool) and one boggy section (after Yeavering Bell)**
Food and drink	**Wooler (shops, café, hotels)**
Summary	**the Way's toughest section, mostly across high moorlands, rewarded by fine views northwards, especially from the track over Gains Law**

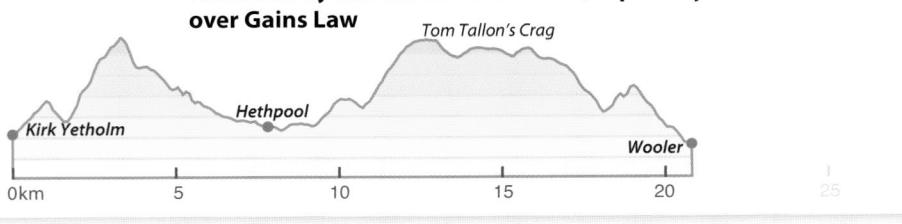

- For the first two miles (3km) of this section, St Cuthbert's Way is also the route of the Pennine Way, with its acorn-logo waymarks: see page 49.

- Take the lane uphill, signed *Halterburn Penial Revival Centre*. It climbs steeply, then descends to Halter Burn glen.

- At the valley floor, bear left along the fence to cross a footbridge with a tall signpost.

- A green path heads uphill, with a wall on its left. At the wall's corner, bear right uphill, around Green Humbleton hill.

- Just above a tin shed, keep ahead as a smaller path crosses diagonally. The main path heads uphill (south-east) on the spur above Green Humbleton, to a signpost announcing the divergence of the Pennine and St Cuthbert's Ways. (Here the Cheviot alternative route separates off: see page 48.)

Above: the Ways diverge
Below: Border ridge, looking back south-west

- Turn left on the path that crosses the slope north-east, rising slightly. It reaches the border fence and wall at a signpost 'Welcome to Scotland/Welcome to England'.

- The grass path continues across the border ridge. Prominent to your left is Eccles Cairn, worth a 5-minute diversion for finer views. (The easiest access is by a trod path off left just sooner than the waymarker, before you descend.)

- The route now descends quite steeply into the valley of Elsdon Burn. Aim for the front bottom corner of a plantation, at the valley floor.

> ### *i* *Kirk Yetholm Gypsies*
> *A law of 1609 made it legal in Scotland to kill Gypsies. Many of the Gypsies retreated to the edge of the hills, where they could find refuge in times of persecution. They are recorded in Kirk Yetholm as early as 1695, including the Gypsy royal family, surnamed Faa. Jean Gordon Faa, the first Gypsy Queen in Kirk Yetholm, inspired the character Meg Merilies in Sir Walter Scott's 1815 novel Guy Mannering. In real life she was banned from Kirk Yetholm for fighting with another woman, and finally was put to death by drowning for supporting the Jacobite Rising. You pass the Gypsie Palace, now a small holiday cottage, on the Way out of Kirk Yetholm.*

- The path crosses a stream to a stile into the plantation near its bottom corner. The route runs under the trees, then along the fence of the plantation bottom, then back under trees again. Where you are uncertain, look out for the tree trunks with their lower branches lopped off.

- A stile leads to open field. Cross this slightly downhill (north-east), to reach a farm track.

- The track ahead fords a stream, rises briefly, then drops to Elsdonburn farm. Zigzag down past the buildings to the start of a tarmac lane.

Descent toward Elsdon Burn

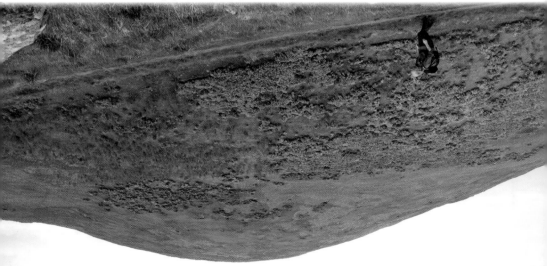

Below Yeavering Bell

- Follow the lane down the valley, ignoring various turnoffs. After 2km join a minor road at a corner and turn right for 300m to Hethpool.
- As the road bends right, turn left (signed 'Old Yeavering') to a bridge over College Burn. At once turn left up a rougher track, that rises and then runs through a plantation to a gate and stile.
- A rough path continues across a field, boggy in places, with more plantations down on your left. Heading north-east you reach a stile into tall gorse bushes.
- Cross a stream, and emerge from the gorse at another stile. Now a faint path slants left, slightly uphill, just north of east (080°), to pass above a stone sheep pen.

- A rough track starts here, running gently uphill and through a plantation. Before Torleehouse take a path on the right just above the track, rejoining the track beyond the house.
- Follow the wide, smooth track for 400m down-valley. Just before a cattle grid, turn off right on a grassy track.

- After 100m the track bends left through a gate. It runs towards a triangular woodland, but bends right, uphill, in front of it.

- The track heads up a grassy spur, but at once there's a gate and ladder stile on the left. Cross onto a wide grassy path that runs uphill, south-east, slanting along the steep side of a rising stream valley. Opposite is the hill fort of Yeavering Bell, with a necklace of fallen stonework around its summit.

- As the path levels off at the valley top, a small cairn and then a waymark post mark a smaller path forking left.

- Ahead, to your left, you'll see the stony outcrop of Tom Tallon's Crag. The Way takes you through the broad col to the right of this.

- At a path junction, bear right along a small path: see photograph below. It heads south-east with unwaymarked posts through the heather below the crag, to a ladder stile.

- Descend to the corner of a track. Follow it ahead, past a plantation on your left, and through a gate.

- The track bends right across a stream. At once turn off left on a grass path (with a small cairn) that soon becomes peaty and boggy.

- The path heads south-east past a tall conical cairn, then gently uphill. Aim towards a skyline wall, but just before it, turn left up a wide track.

- The track follows the wall and then passes through it at a gate, to join a wider track. (This track gives easy moorland walking for the next 4km, and perhaps your first views of the sea ahead.)

- Follow this new track ahead (north-east) along a long moorland hump; the wall is on your left at first, then turns away.

Path junction: the Way bears right here

- At the hump's end, the track crosses a narrower col, where it bends right. Now the track runs south-east around the flank of Gains Law. To the left is Humbleton Hill.

- Stay on the track as it bends left and passes the end of a wide moorland hump to a gate.

- Through the gate, heather ground gives way to grassland. The track bends slightly right (south-east) and descends gradually around the northern flank of Coldberry Hill.

> *i* **Humbleton Hill**
> Humbleton Hill has an Iron Age hill fort. If you divert over it, you can drop down to Humbleton village for a short-cut into Wooler. The hill was the site of a battle in 1402 between two great Border families: the Percies of Northumberland and the Douglases of Scotland. The Scots' defeat was recorded by Shakespeare, who refers to the battle as Holmedon (Henry IV Part 1).
> A steep grassy hollow separates Humbleton Hill from the moorland crossed by the Way. This 'meltwater channel' is the course carved by a small river in the Ice Age, when its natural run-off to the north was blocked by ice.

- The Way bends left and descends more steeply to go through a gate. At once, turn right off the good track. Another gate leads to a grassy path running east.

- After 300m the path bends right, to a gate at the top of a plantation. An earth path leads down through it to a tarmac one, where you turn right into the car park at Wooler Common. (The road to the left, Common Road, is a short-cut into Wooler, but this misses out some fairly impressive earthworks.)

- Out of the car park turn right, at once forking left at a signpost just before a stream. A path leads upstream, with forest on its left, for 300m.

- At the wood corner the path turns uphill through gorse. You are aiming for the top corner of the same plantation but the direct path there is not a right-of-way; so fork right (south) to meet a fence.

- Turn sharp left and descend beside the fence to a gate at the plantation corner. The path now runs uphill, with trees on its left and then on both sides, to a clearing.

- Follow the path ahead along the clearing, then downhill through the trees to a gate out of the plantation. The grassy path continues ahead, with the earthworks of the Kettles on its right.

- The path wanders downhill into a reed-filled valley, where it bends left to the drive-way of Waud Hause. The track leads down to Common Road at the edge of Wooler.

North-east over Wooler

- Turn right along the street. As it turns downhill, it becomes Ramsey's Lane. (Here a bridleway path on the right contours round to the youth hostel.)
- Otherwise the street leads down into Wooler's Market Square. The Way continues diagonally opposite, down Church Street.

St Mary's Church, Wooler

Wooler's name probably means 'well on the hill', and it has been settled since the Stone Age. The Kettles, the Iron Age settlement just above the town, was reused by the Romans, and many cup-and-ring marked rocks are to the east. Wooler's first recorded mention is in 1107: 'situated in an ill-cultivated country under the influence of vast mountains, from whence it is subject to impetuous rains'. It has been a busy market town since its charter was granted in 1199.

Lying so close both to the hills and to the border, it suffered severely in the reiving times, being attacked by Scots in both 1340 and 1409. The town was garrisoned at various times by both nations: the earthworks of its timber castle remain above Church Street.

Street names such as *Tenter Hill* underline the importance of Wooler's weaving trade. 'Tenters' are frames on which the woven cloth is stretched out after weaving. Wooler's large number of inns suggest its former importance on the turnpike road to Scotland, now bypassed by the A1. Its community website is at ***www.wooler.org.uk***.

High Street, Wooler

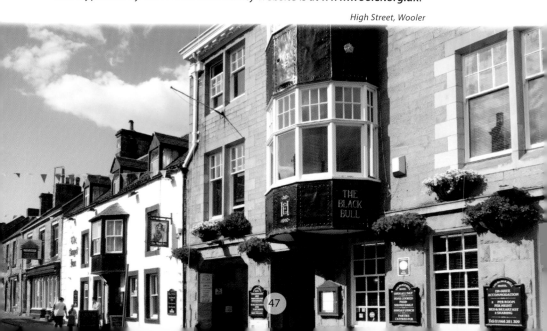

3·3b The Cheviot alternative

Map	**panels 2 and 3**
Distance	**18 miles (29 km)**
Terrain	**hill paths, most of which are firm and dry, with stone-paved paths over Cheviot summit. The descent is on peaty paths, hill tracks and a quiet road**
Food and drink	**none until Wooler: there's a refuge hut at Auchope Rig**
Summary	**hill crossing over the high-point of eastern England, more serious and strenuous than anything on the official Way**

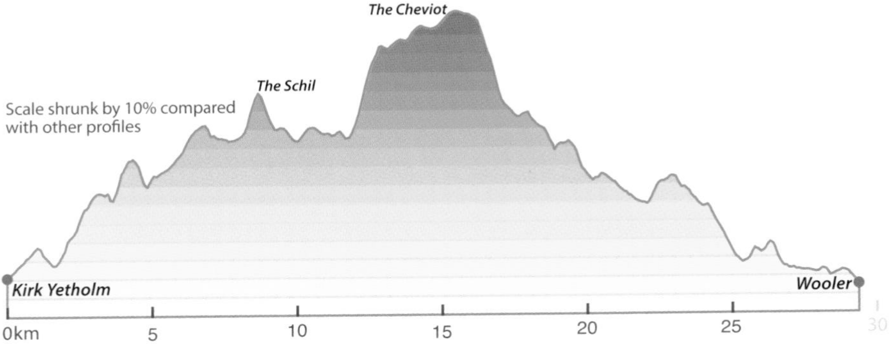

The Cheviot

The Schil

Scale shrunk by 10% compared with other profiles

Kirk Yetholm   *Wooler*

0km   5   10   15   20   25   30

• See page 42: from Kirk Yetholm, follow the Way for two miles (3km) to the signpost where St Cuthbert's and Pennine Ways diverge. (From here, this option follows the Pennine Way all the way to the summit of the Cheviot.)

• Keep uphill to a wall and fence on the ridgeline. The grassy path follows the fence to the right (south), into a sharp dip and then up to the col between the two summits of White Law.

Descending White Law toward Steer Rig

- Cross a ladder stile and follow the wall to the left, to the main top of White Law. Continue to right of the fence, down across a col and up the gentle ridge of Steer Rig, to a gate west of Black Hag's summit.

- Ignoring the summit just up to your left, keep ahead, slightly downhill, to join a wider path at a signpost. This path bends gradually to the left, to rejoin the ridgeline wall south of Black Hag.

- Cross another stile, and turn right alongside the wall. After passing across a heathery col, the wall becomes a fence which leads up, past a rocky tor, to the Schil. The Schil's summit tor is to the right of the fence.

Pennine Way waymarker

- Keep to the left of the fence as you continue over a minor hump called Birnie Brae. The fence and ridgeline now turn left (east) and rise slightly to the Auchope Shelter Hut. Useful in emergencies, the wooden hut is cold and uncomfortable and lacks a convenient water supply.

- Continue beside the fence up to Auchope Cairn, with its two square cairns. A wood-slatted path leads across the peaty plateau for 800m, to a three-way Pennine Way signpost on the main Cheviot ridgeline.

Tor just below the Schil summit

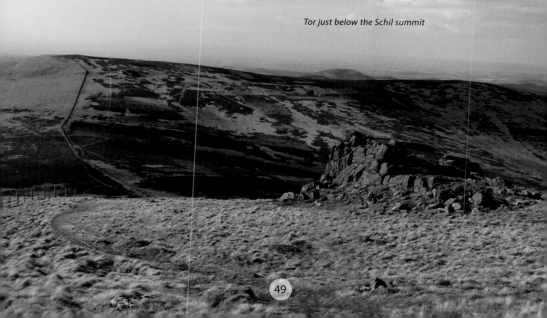

The Cheviot from Windy Gyle

- Turn left (north-east), on a stone-slabbed path. A fence joins from the right for the final climb to the scruffy shelter cairn of Cairn Hill.

- Keep the fence on your right, and follow the stone-slabbed path. It rises gently (still north-east) to the trig point of the Cheviot at 815m (2674ft).

- Continue along the slabbed path east, to cross a ladder stile at the plateau edge. Turn left, now with the fence on your left. This fence, to the left of the path, will guide you for the next 3km.

- The small, grassy path descends roughly north-east, becoming stony as the descent steepens. It crosses a long col, and rises slightly to a stile on Scald Hill.

- The path and fence continue down ahead. As the slope steepens, the path and fence bend slightly left (north) to cross the head of a narrow valley.

- The path and fence ascend steeply out of the little valley, then level off on the shoulder of Broadhope Hill. Before the ground rises again, fork right on a peaty path through the heather (north-east). This is where you finally leave the useful guiding fence.

The Cheviot summit

- The path bends slightly right, and dips into the stream valley of Hawsen Burn. Keeping to left of the stream, it passes the end of a grassy track running to the left.

- The small, waymarked path runs just above the stream, then rejoins the track just above. Continue along the track until it joins a larger, gravel-surfaced one. (For a more sheltered way to Wooler, turn down to the right – the track follows Hawsen Burn down to the Harthope Burn valley, where the tarmac road leads out to Earle and Wooler.)

- Turn sharp left up the new track, through the col between Broadhope Hill and Cold Law. The track heads down the valley of Hazelly Burn (roughly north), to a track junction.

- Ignore the side-track left, and follow the main track across the north flank of Cold Law. The track rises slightly to a gate, then runs down the steep spur (north-east) to Harthope Burn.

- Turn left along the tarmac valley road. After 750m it rises left, away from the river, then drops to a junction beside Middleton Hall.

- Turn left, signposted 'Wooler'. Follow the lane through Earle, and at a slightly larger road bear left.

- The road passes Wooler Youth Hostel, then descends Cheviot Street to Wooler's Market Square. St Cuthbert's Way continues diagonally left, down Church Street.

i **Cheviot volcano**

The Cheviot is a lump of granite. About 10km wide, this is a magma lump that cooled deep underground, and is now exposed by the erosion of the massive volcanoes that stood on top. The pink, crystalline granite is seen on Cheviot summit and the descent. On the way up to it, the stones you'll see are pinkish rhyolite, sprinkled with yellow crystals of feldspar. This rhyolite is the same stuff as the granite, but squeezed out as dykes into the surrounding country. Because it cooled more quickly, it lacks the granite's crystals.

The granite and rhyolite are harder than the surrounding sandstones, which is why the Cheviots stand high above the lowlands to north and south.

Across Bowmont Water to the Border ridge

3·4 Wooler to Fenwick

Map	**panel 3 and page 64**
Distance	**12 miles (19.5 km)**
Terrain	**good paths, tracks, and minor roads**
Food and drink	**Wooler only (shops, café, hotels)**
Summary	**a gentle mix of moorland, pastureland and forest, with a possible lunch stop at Cuthbert's Cave, and your first clear view of Lindisfarne**

Wooler — St Cuthbert's Cave — *Fenwick*

0km — 5 — 10 — 15 — 20 — 25

- From Wooler's Market Place, head down Church Street past St Mary's Church to South Road (the A697). Cross the river by a steel arch bridge.

- At once, turn right past the bowling green, on a lane which becomes a footpath along the backs of houses by the river. At the next road (Weetwood Avenue), turn left across the wide Glendale valley.

- The road ascends and bends firmly to the right. Here take a footpath on the left, uphill to the top of Weetwood Moor. (Across the moorland, to the right of the Way, is a cup-and-ring marked rock: see panel on page 53.)

- The wide, grassy path runs north-east along the moorland rim. Pass along the right edge of a plantation, towards a second one.

- At the front corner of this next plantation turn left alongside it. Head diagonally to a kissing-gate at the corner of another plantation, then turn downhill to its right.

- The path bends right to a small gate into newly planted woodland. It slants down through the growing trees, and across a field below, to a ladder stile at Weetwood Bridge.

Cup and ring marked rocks, Weetwood Moor

- Cross the bridge, and after 500m fork right for 'Hortons, Lowick'. Follow the lane for 2km to East Horton (B&B here), where you turn left, signed for 'Lowick, Ancroft'.

- After 500m turn right on a tarmac track north-east. After it passes a World War 2 pillbox, it descends for 800m on a gravelly surface. At the bottom, bear left on the main track, which crosses Hetton Burn and then rises to a junction.

- Take the lane ahead signed Belford, past the Old Schoolhouse (another B&B). 50m after a side road on the right, turn left on a green track.

- Within 100m pass a small quarry, then turn up right through a gate. Turn left along the field foot, roughly north, following the line of a fence to the field corner. (A plantation strip runs uphill just above this point.)

> **Cup and ring marked rock**
> Cup-and-ring marks probably date from the late Stone Age. Nobody knows their meaning or function. The sandstone of Weetwood Moor has several, one only 250m from the Way – though finding it takes careful searching (or a GPS).
> As the Way levels at the moorland plateau, there's a waymarked path junction. From this point head south past two boulders at the moor top. Once the nearby radio mast lies directly south-west, start looking for a flat-topped rock. Alternatively, if you have a GPS, set it to NU 01020 28020.
> As several thousand years of wind and rain have been eroding the markings, they are best seen under the low sun of morning or evening.

Descent toward Weetwood Bridge

Approaching St Cuthbert's Cave

- Continue with a hedge to your left, down to a complicated junction. Here turn sharp right, up a track that starts on gravel, then turns grassy, to the foot of the wooded steeper slope above.

- Turn left along the plantation foot, then continue just inside it. A path runs up right, towards St Cuthbert's Cave: see panel. If you follow this to the cave, you need not backtrack but can cross a stile up on the left out of the wood.

- However, the Way bypasses the cave, keeping ahead along the plantation edge to its bottom corner. Just outside, it turns right, uphill.

> ### *i* St Cuthbert's Cave
> The cave is a natural one, eroded out of yellow Fell Sandstone, standing in a mature pine wood. It has room to shelter several people.
> Escaping the Danish raid of AD875, Bishop Eardulf of Lindisfarne and the monks carried St Cuthbert's body around Britain for seven years. According to legend, this cave was one of their first stops. The body then visited Cumberland, south-west Scotland, Ripon in Yorkshire and even Melrose, Cuthbert's early home. When it was placed on a ship at Whitehaven, with the intention of carrying it across to Ireland, a rain of blood from the sky indicated that the saint should not be removed. His body eventually found a safe resting place at Durham.

- The Way runs up alongside the pine wood to its top corner. Here it turns left through a gate at the ridgeline, and at once left again through a narrower one. Here is your first clear view ahead of Lindisfarne island and its castle.

- A short diversion up to the left here gains Greensheen Hill. It's a good spot for picnics, rocky scrambles, and even for geology.

- From the two gates the path heads downhill, north-east, gradually diverging from a fence on the right to cross a footbridge. Cross the next field on the same heading to a gate, then bend left to another gate with signpost, onto a track.

- Turn left, signed 'Holburn'. The track bends north-west with a fence on its right, to enter forest plantations. Hummocks of former coal mining are to the right of the track before the forest.

- After 100m, turn right on a forest track that bends left again to run northwards. Ignore all side-tracks and descend on the main track into cleared ground. Now the track bends right, but the Way takes a narrow path ahead, still northward.

- The small path crosses a track, eventually emerging to a field corner at a stile. The path continues north for almost 2km, with the wood on its left and open fields running gently down to the coast on the right.

- At the wood corner, the path runs ahead with a hedge on its left for one field. It turns left through a field gate, and runs with a hedge on its right to a lane, alongside a house called Blawearie.

- Turn right for 800m, and follow the lane down to Fenwick.

Fenwick has several B&Bs, but an early tide may mean you prefer to spend the night closer to the causeway, at or near Beal. In that case, turn left in Fenwick (instead of right to follow the Way), and at the village edge take the lane on the right. This runs directly to the A1 at Beal Road End (filling station with shop, Lindisfarne Inn and buses to Berwick). Keep ahead for Beal (B&Bs) and the Lindisfarne causeway.

St Cuthbert's Cave

3·5 Fenwick to Lindisfarne

Map	**page 64**
Distance	**6 miles (9.5 km)**
Terrain	**field paths and causeway (or tidal mud on Pilgrims' Path)**
Food and drink	**none until Holy Island village (shop, hotels, cafés)**
Summary	**a short field section leads to the extraordinary crossing of Beal Sands to the Holy Island of Lindisfarne**

Fenwick
Holy Island

0km   5   10   15   20   25

- Turn right in the village and cross the busy A1 trunk road with care, into a lane which you follow for 500m. After Granary Bank, turn left up a hedged track.

- At the top, the track turns right, bending back north again to another lane. Turn right for 100m, then turn left down the edge of a field, to the railway crossing.

- Use the yellow phone to speak with the signalman before crossing. He may ask you to wait for a few minutes if a high-speed train is approaching. When it's safe, cross the railway lines with care.

- Go straight on to a path continuing north-east, to a footbridge over a drainage ditch. Fork left to cross a field diagonally to a gate at its far corner.

- Bear right on a track running north. Where it bends left, bear off right on a grass path across a field to the shoreline with its concrete anti-tank blocks. If you've timed your tides right, there's probably hardly any sea in view.

- Turn left between the rows of anti-tank blocks, to the road and car park at the end of the Lindisfarne causeway. Check the safe crossing times shown on the signboard here.

- Turn right along the causeway across the mudflats, to the refuge shelter on stilts where the causeway crosses a permanent river.

Railway crossing with phone

If it is safe, here you can turn off the busy road to the Pilgrims' Path across the sand and mud: see page 11 for how to decide whether time and tide permit.

Otherwise follow the road along its causeway to the sand dunes of Lindisfarne. Walk around its bay to pass the large car park at the north edge of Holy Island village.

Follow the road into the village to a T-junction where the priory is ahead. This is the official end of the Way. To reach the castle, continue for a further 800m to the left.

i **Pilgrims' Path**

More adventurous and romantic, from the bridge and refuge shelter, is to follow tall poles that mark the Pilgrims' Path across the sands. For 1500 years until the building of the road causeway, this was the only route to Holy Island. The marker poles and refuge shelters were raised in the 1990s. Bare feet are best. Most of the going is firm but there will be usually be some short sections of oozy mud, as well as shallow pools and streams to wade through. The Pilgrims' Path rejoins the road just north of Holy Island village.

Causeway with rescue tower, dawn

Lindisfarne

Lindisfarne Priory

Lindisfarne is the Saxon name: *farne* means 'retreat', but probably a retreat from dangerous enemies rather than a religious one. Since the time of Cuthbert, it has been known as Holy Island. Today its formal title is 'the Holy Island of Lindisfarne'.

The island's resident population is less than 200. Today it is a place of pilgrimage not only for Christians, but also for naturalists, bird-watchers and archeologists. Over 500,000 people visit each year, and 50,000 birds over-winter here.

Cuthbert's priory is now a roofless ruin, with stone columns reaching upwards towards the sky. North Sea breezes blowing through the high arches have furrowed the soft sandstone, the wind erosion obvious after just a few short centuries.

A statue of St Aidan, the priory's founder, stands outside the entrance. Behind it is a tall cross that could be considered the final waymark of St Cuthbert's Way. There's an entry fee for the priory itself, but the surrounding graveyard is accessible at any time. At its end, next to the shore, is a modern statue of St Cuthbert.

Nearby in Holy Island village is the Lindisfarne Centre. Here is a beautiful replica of the Lindisfarne Gospels, the original being held at the British Library. There is a display on the Viking raid of AD793, and an introduction to the wildlife and ecology of the island.

As you head out of the village to the harbour, you come across a line of old fishing boats, inverted and painted with pitch for waterproofing. These are used as stores by the Lindisfarne fishermen. The harbour itself is tidal, with bare mud at low water. It is used mainly by pleasure yachts.

Beyond rises Lindisfarne Castle. It was built in 1550, using stones looted from the Priory ruins, to guard the harbour. Early in the 20th century it was converted to a family home by the architect Edwin Lutyens (designer of New Delhi and of the Cenotaph in London). He used the natural textures of stone, slate and timber to atmospheric effect. To north of the castle is the walled garden created for it by the famous designer Gertrude Jekyll. It has recently been restored to its original planting scheme.

East of the castle are handsome Victorian limekilns. The island's limestone was processed here before being carried away by boat for use in the fields and in making mortar for building. Onwards to the north lie the 10km of sand dunes and salt marsh and tidal mud, the island's unique wildlife zone. The rare plants, seals and tens of thousands of birds have been described briefly in Section 2·3. To study them in full could take a lifetime.

After four, five, or six days of walking, Lindisfarne is a place to stand still – to gaze across the North Sea at sunrise, to watch the sea mist threading through the high arch of the Priory, to see the tide creep inwards and the sea-birds move up towards you across the mud.

i **Lindisfarne opening times**
Opening hours vary to suit the causeway crossing times. The castle (National Trust) is open 10.00 to 15.00 or 12.00 to 17.00. The Lindisfarne Centre is generally open 10.00 to 17.00 (in season). The Priory may be open 10.00 to 16.00, causeway permitting, with midweek closures October to February. Check online for causeway crossing times: www.lindisfarne.org.uk.

Lindisfarne Castle from the village

4 Reference

Useful websites

The official website is *www.stcuthbertsway.info* and is worth checking for any route changes.

Ranger service

Three authorities maintain and manage the Way. Contact the relevant one to report problems with access/waymarking or to appreciate their work:

Melrose to English Border: Scottish Borders Council Ranger Service   01835 826 509
   outdooraccess@scotborders.co.uk

English Border to Wooler Common:
Northumberland National Park Authority
   enquiries@nnpa.org.uk   01434 605 555

Wooler to Lindisfarne: Northumberland County Council Countryside   0345 600 6400
   countryside@northumberland.gov.uk

Weather

For weather forecasts:
   www.metoffice.gov.uk
   www.bbc.co.uk.weather

Forecasts are also posted daily in youth hostels and some information centres. You can also listen to local radio.

Mountain Weather Information Systems
   www.mwis.org.uk: their Southern Uplands forecast covers the Cheviots.

Lindisfarne causeway tide times

   http://bit.ly/SCWtides or call   01289 330 733
(Berwick TIC) for tide times, which are also posted on the door at Wooler TIC and at the mainland end of the causeway.

Maps: printed and online

Harvey Maps publishesd an XT40 (polythene) edition of their 1:40,000 whole-route map in 2014 (978-1-85137-474-8):

   www.harveymaps.co.uk. For the Cheviot diversion, we recommend Ordnance Survey's sheet OL16 (*www.ordnancesurvey.co.uk*). Our online route map is at

   www.rucsacs.com/routemap/scw and shows both the Way and several routes from Tweedbank: zoom in for amazing detail.

Access

In Scotland, everyone has the right to be on most land and inland water providing that they act responsibly: see

   www.outdooraccess-scotland.com
where you can download varioius Scottish Natural Heritage publications: the full *Scottish Outdoor Access Code* is offered as an ebook or PDF. The leaflet *Enjoy Scotland's Outdoors* provides a summary of the Code and there's a leaflet specially for *Dog Owners*.

In England, the whole of the route runs on rights of way, but much of the upland ground alongside it is open access land, marked by a 'brown walker' waymark. For details, visit

   www.naturalengland.org.uk and search for *open access land*.

Visitor information

   www.visitnorthumberland.com is the official Northumberland Tourism site.

   www.discovertheborders.co.uk is an independent commercial site about the area.

   www.northumberlandnationalpark.org.uk covers the Northumberland National Park section of the Way.

   www.lindisfarne.org.uk **is** Holy Island's own site with accommodation, information, and causeway times.

   www.onlineborders.org.uk provides local and community information for the area.

   www.returntotheridings.co.uk has details on the Common Ridings.

Information Centres

Melrose (April–October), Priorwood Garden, Abbey St, Melrose TD6 9PX   01896 822 283

Harestanes Country Visitor Centre (April–October), Ancrum, Jedburgh TD8 6UQ
                                          01835 830 306

Jedburgh (all year), Murray's Green, Jedburgh, TD8 6BE   01835 863 170

Kirk Yetholm unmanned information point at Border Hotel

Wooler (closed winter weekdays), The Cheviot Centre, Wooler NE71 6BL   01668 282 123

Berwick-upon-Tweed (all year)   01289 330 733
106 Marygate, Berwick-upon-Tweed TD15 1BN for information on Northumberland.

Places of Interest

Melrose Abbey, Dryburgh Abbey, Jedburgh Abbey:
www.historic-scotland.gov.uk
In 2016, opening hours (for all three) were 9.30-17.30 from Easter to the end of September, and 10.00-16.00 October to March. Adult admission cost £5.50 (£4.40 concession).

Mary Queen of Scots Visitor Centre, Jedburgh
01835 863 331

Three Hills Roman Heritage Centre, Melrose
www.trimontium.org.uk

Monteviot House
www.monteviot.com

Lindisfarne Castle
www.nationaltrust.org.uk

Lindisfarne Priory
www.english-heritage.org.uk

Lindisfarne National Nature Reserve
www.naturalengland.org.uk

The Lindisfarne Centre
www.lindisfarne-centre.com

Farne Islands

Seahouses Information Centre 01665 720 884 (closed Nov–March) Seafield Road, Seahouses

Billy Shiel's Farne Island Boat Trips
www.farne-islands.com   01665 720 308.

Service providers

For accommodation booking with baggage transport, consider Walking Support:
Walking Support
www.walkingsupport.co.uk   0189 682 2079
For the Easter group walking pilgrimage to Holy Island, see Northern Cross
www.northerncross.co.uk
For a range of other packaged options, please visit
www.rucsacs.com/books/scw.

Transport

For international journey planning, try
www.rome2rio.com
Traveline journey planners cover travel between towns, cities, rail stations and airports throughout the UK:
www.traveline.info

For travel within the north of England:
www.travelinenortheast.info
and within Scotland
www.travelinescotland.com
The train service between Edinburgh and Tweedbank (near Melrose) is provided by ScotRail:
www.scotrail.co.uk
The journey takes under an hour and leaves twice hourly between about 06.00 and midnight (hourly on Sundays, between about 09.00 and 23.00).

Scottish Citylink:
www.citylink.co.uk   0871 266 3333
National Express:
www.nationalexpress.com   0871 781 8181
For Lindisfarne bus timetables:
www.lindisfarne.org.uk

Newcastle Airport
www.newcastleairport.com

Edinburgh Airport
www.edinburghairport.com

Youth hostels

There are two hostels very close to the route: both are open to individuals from March to November (groups may occupy them in winter months). Membership is optional and there's no upper age limit. Sheets are provided and basic meals may be available. Expect to pay about £18 a night (adult) for a bed in a shared dormitory. You can book Kirk Yetholm's Friends of Nature House (01573 420 639) via the SYHA website. For the Wooler hostel and Shepherds' Huts, use the YHA website.

Scottish Youth Hostels Association
www.syha.org.uk   0345 293 7373
Youth Hostels Association
www.yha.org.uk   01629 592 700

Recommended reading

For those tackling the Way in sections, we recommend *St Cuthbert's Way: 24 Short Walks* which describes walks ranging from 1-8 miles along and around the Way, many of them circular. The book is spiral bound, costs £9.99 (+p&p) and can be bought from *www.stcuthbertsway.info*.

Pronunciation guide

Berwick	berrick
Bowden	bow rhymes with cow
Cheviot	cheeviot
Earle	yearl
Eildon	eeldon
Fenwick	fennick
Hownam	hoonam
Teviot	teeviot
Yeavering Bell	yevvering bell
Yetholm	yettum

Acknowledgements

We thank Ron Shaw and Roger Smith for collaborating to devise the Way, which opened in 1996. Thanks also to the ranger services mentioned on p60 for their work in maintaining the Way. We thank three individuals for commenting on drafts: Phil Bradley (Northumberland County Council), John Henderson (*www.walkingsupport.co.uk*) and Neil Mackay (Scottish Borders Council Ranger Service). The author thanks David Howard for company along the walk.

Rucksack Readers

All our guidebooks are rainproof, robust and lightweight, written by walkers for walkers.

Photo credits

Berwickshire News p15 (lower); **Durham Cathedral** p19; istockphoto/**Alistair Scott** p18; istockphoto/**Herbert Kratk**y p26 middle; istockphoto/**topshotUK** p28 upper; **Neil Mackay** p12 (all); **Jacquetta Megarry** p9, p13, p15 upper, p21 upper, p22, p27 lower, p28 lower, p29 (both), p34 lower, p35, p45, p46, p47 both; **Sandy Morrison** p24; **Gordon Simm** p27 (inset); all other photographs, including front and back covers, by **Ronald Turnbull**.

Altitude profiles credit: Mapyx Ltd

The publisher thanks Mapyx for supplying all the altitude profiles from Quo, its award-winning free digital mapping software. Mapyx Quo can be downloaded free from *www.mapyx.com.*

Notes for novices

We offer advice on preparation and gear: follow the *Notes for novices* link from *www.rucsacs.com.*

Rucksack Readers has published books covering long-distance walks in Scotland, England, Ireland and worldwide (the Alps, China, Peru and Tanzania). Its series *Rucksack Pocket Summits* is for climbers of the world's 'seven summits'. For more information, or to order online, visit *www.rucsacs.com.* To order by telephone, dial 0131 661 0262 (outside UK dial +44 131 661 0262).

Index

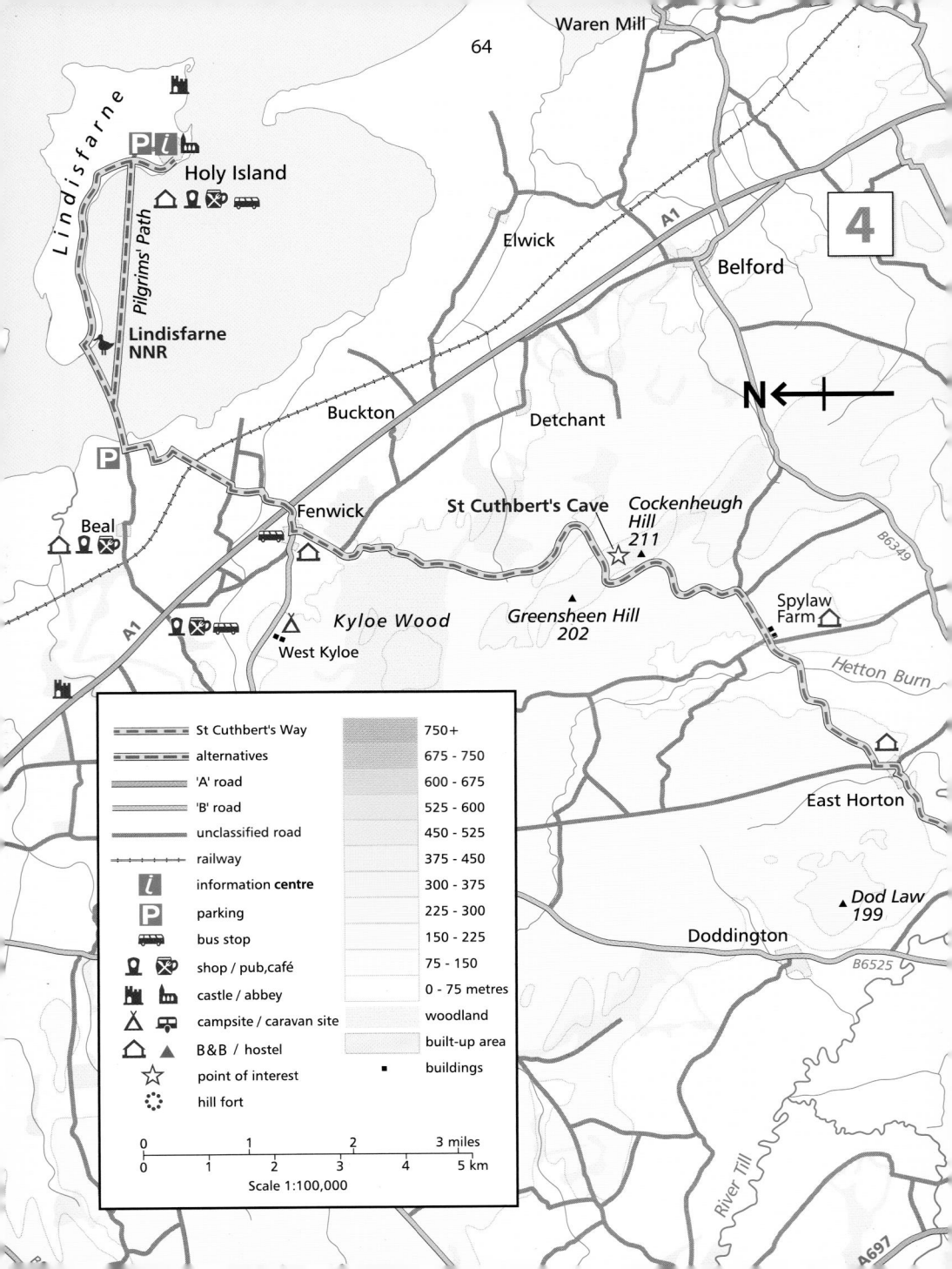

Waren Mill

Lindisfarne

Holy Island

Pilgrims' Path

Lindisfarne
NNR

Elwick

A1

Belford

4

N

Buckton

Detchant

P

Beal

Fenwick

St Cuthbert's Cave

*Cockenheugh
Hill
211*

A1

West Kyloe

Kyloe Wood

*Greensheen Hill
202*

Spylaw
Farm

B6349

Hetton Burn

East Horton

*Dod Law
199*

Doddington

B6525

River Till

A697

St Cuthbert's Way		750+
alternatives		675 - 750
'A' road		600 - 675
'B' road		525 - 600
unclassified road		450 - 525
railway		375 - 450
i	information **centre**	300 - 375
P	parking	225 - 300
	bus stop	150 - 225
	shop / pub,café	75 - 150
	castle / abbey	0 - 75 metres
	campsite / caravan site	woodland
	B&B / hostel	built-up area
☆	point of interest	■ buildings
	hill fort	

0   1   2   3 miles
0   1   2   3   4   5 km
Scale 1:100,000